MW01046333

I AM THE BIG HEART

I AM THE BIG HEART

SARAH VENART

BRICK BOOKS

Library and Archives Canada Cataloguing in Publication

Title: I am the big heart / Sarah Venart.
Names: Venart, Sarah, 1968- author.
Description: Poems.
Identifiers: Canadiana (print) 20200220535 | Canadiana (ebook) 2020022056X | ISBN 9781771315364 (softcover) | ISBN 9781771315371 (HTML) | ISBN 9781771315388 (PDF)
Classification: LCC PS8643.E53 I2 2020 | DDC C811/.6—dc23

We acknowledge the Canada Council for the Arts, the Government of Canada through the Canada Book Fund, and the Ontario Arts Council for their support of our publishing program.

The author photo was taken by Cristina Lugo.
The book is set in Scala.
The cover image is *Carey*, by Janet Werner.
Designed by Marijke Friesen.
Printed and bound by Coach House Printing.

Brick Books
487 King St. W.
Kingston, ON
K7L 2X7

www.brickbooks.ca

For Joanne, Catherine, Jennifer, Michael, Madelaine, and Emily

It is called feeling but is its real name thought?
—Denise Riley

CONTENTS

JOY IN THE CLOISTERS

THE BIG HEART

Epiphany

Here I am, with one hour to find it.
Here I am in this tenth month, the peeler of pears,
the slicer of hot dogs, cutting them into strips
smaller than a child's windpipe.
Here's my apologetic smile, accepted by the daycare
in return for my children. So what is there to find
in one hour on my desk's shallow surface?
I've mislaid all of it somewhere among
my mind's tiny grey flags, in the millions of scraps
piling up. I left it behind in the dark bleeding gums
of the dog that I loved, watching her clench yet another rock
from the tide. That was twelve years ago.
What was she looking for?
What if she'd stopped looking?
Metaphors were easy then, not only the sky,
but migrating everywhere. And now everyone is arrow
arrow, arrows. Everyone harpoons.
And I am the big heart, aren't I?
When my black dog was being put down, in her last
second I whispered, *Squirrel*.

Attenborough

First month of kindergarten, out of the blue,
slabs appear at the bottom of her artwork.
Ocean, she informs me. A second wedge
appears, light blue, a sky in which a two-inch kea
soars downward for his lunch: red stripe of fish on a box
with wheels and windows. *I am the smartest animal*
on earth, she chants. *I am the smartest animal.*
Okay, I concede. But to debate her thesis,
I press play on YouTube, where birds of paradise
do the work of pop-up pomp,
firework faces appearing on the black stage
of their wings. *They're puppets,* she bluffs.
But! The strongest muscle in my body is my tongue!
Just like that, she flutters off to the mirror down the hall
where her reflection flips a glittering headband
back and forth between its palms.
It's best if I stay hidden behind the laundry basket.
Bowerbird! she's singing, her quick hands ruffling the air—
Giraffes can clean their ears with their tongue,
this infant human says to her reflection
before she shapes her fingers into a heart
using her twenty-nine hand bones.

Walk to School

My daughter runs into the wet light of morning.
She'll want to use the iron rail up ahead

as a tightrope. If I don't let her
we'll risk the siren windup of the scream,

the plump collapse on sidewalk.
Feelings must be heard, I've learned, so I overhear

my daughter's crayoned frantic faces on leg sticks
as code for *love now, love more.*

The errant hair clip flapping forward in her hair
means *leave me be.*

As the dog worries after groundhogs,
my daughter pushes through

seedling weed maples, boots wetted by the spurs
of sward.

She chants up ahead with a sting in her tail:
I hate dew, I hate dew, I hate dew—

The Chauffeur

I look up and it's time to go. All ambulance, I fetch
one daughter at daycare, the other at kindergarten,

though I'm too early. So I see the heartbreak—
class lights out, the children, even mine,

small heads laid out on desks waiting
for the signal of dismissal. Even so, we are let go.

And even though so many signs
discourage us, one bearded father slows his car

in the middle of the street and leans past
his steering wheel to ask me

about camp registration. I open the back door
to buckle someone in. Then I buckle someone else.

Is his the last call into the backwoods
of my radiance? I grip the door handle

as the wasteland between my hips fills rapidly—
I don't know how to stop myself

from turning to answer him, flowing
from domestic into feral

just like that.

The Midwife Advises Me

To go rogue, stop holding onto
what hurts, indulge in this minute, make
room for what's good.

I eat deli meat rolled into fat cigars.
No raw food, no shellfish! The sushi chef
shakes his wet finger when I pop in

to stop holding on to what hurts. One more
Edomae, Saint-Honoré cheese, a raw rind
I break open with the spoon,

making room for what's good.
I eat my way through it, indulge
in this minute, worm my way into joy.

Or not joy. *Stop holding on,*
just stop. I know better—umbilically
speaking—below my own gut, inside the womb

you nurture yourself, making room
for what's better. You're a mystery
growing placidly despite the metallic taunt

of that last lobster roll. *Go rogue, make room.*
Stop holding on to the rules. You come out
four weeks too early. We are not good

with rules. When I'm asked not to push, I turn myself
inside out to make room for what I hope
will be better. From my mercurial nest, out you

coil. You're quiet and jaundiced with questions:
Why hold on to what hurts? The blue milk
of your eyes says, *Make room for what's good.*

This Strange Thing Happened the Day You Were Born

The woman in the bed across the room appears
to be on hormonal hallucinogens.

Not counting toes and fingers
on her own sleeping baby,

she's fixed on the thin ribbed mauve of your chest.
I'm fixed on you too, the submerged navy moons

of your eyes. I should be alarmed
when she asks, *Can I hold her?*

But I let her hold you.
She stares down at your face.

I watch you watch back:
what was danger before now?

Before this everything
was off the cuff, diary entry, pop song, kitsch dish, frost warning.

The Difficult Ones

I'd been having problems, so I made an appointment
to return to Sinclair the midwife. I needed her
one more time to teach me, or my baby, to latch on.

In the sunlit dream of her office, in the easy chair,
an afghan and a pillow propping my arm, Sinclair
stood behind me, used her palm and this indulgent voice
reserved for babies, and she got us latched.

Between us, my baby swallowed silky mouthfuls
at my breast. Latching was so easy with Sinclair.
I had a vision in that plush chair: I'd be able to go it alone

on the fussy evening feed tonight, I was planted now
with the wisdom of the palm, the pinkie, and Sinclair's
voice in my head. How grateful, how tired I was

when I thanked her, shakily: *I'll never forget you.*
Nor I you, said Sinclair. Her hands clapped onto the knees
of her colourful scrubs as she added: *You always remember the difficult ones—*

I forget almost everything else about the birth: how long
I pushed, was the water around me really a cesspool, did I climb
from the tub, did I wash or sleep? If my stitches had broken,

or I'd complained about how I'd been sewn up,
that to me would be difficult. Had I sworn at her
during the labour's transition from woman to mammal,

okay. If they'd needed the big fish sieve to clean up my pool—
I couldn't remember. Everything I'd been so sure
I'd been before—affable, even gracious in my first trimester,

smiling benignly when, with her fingers inside me,
Sinclair had pushed at the wall between one part of me and another
and suggested I needed more fibre?

I wanted to be carried back a minute to that warmer armchair.
Sinclair had helped me then, unclipping my bra cup
before transporting my fussing newborn with her tiny chafed pout
onto the firebox of my breast and fixing us, the difficult ones, into place.

Origami

At night I close my eyes and let my thoughts
become my feelings, let my feelings point their corners

into dark corners. I fold the word *daughter*
over and over until it contains the word *duty*.

I've heard there's a Kenyan tribe that makes paper
by filling their mouths with dust and water.

They flatten that paste onto stones and fold it
into envelopes they send to Japan

where eleven-year-old Siberian girls
wait in tiny pleated apartments to be models.

I pull at the skin and the fat
on my hip bones, and the bones beneath

become sharp as hangers. Watching a thing
become another thing makes me hopeful: watching string

turn into the Eiffel tower
with only three fingers and a mouth pulling up its peak

is a mystery I should write down.
Instead, I'm here on my bed in the dark

watching this girl on YouTube demonstrate
Jacob's ladder, witch's broom, cat's cradle.

Her hands are so deft. Her transformations effortless.
In real time they twist away and vanish.

Fox's Sleep

The first pill gives you sleep like warm butter.

Then it leaves the butter dish out.

Then it moves the butter dish to

                                  not where you've left it.

Murmuration Digression

Over bedtime chia pudding, my four-year-old informs me
    that I am not her favourite.
            She prefers her father
    though he doesn't let her wade in puddles after heavy rains.
Her preference slips so easily from her mouth
into the lit oasis of our kitchen island.   I crunch to a halt.
    Carry myself   to the dusk and darkness
    of the stove,   pretend   to polish knobs.
    I am a floating object,   a tectonic plate
        who scoops noodles from the floor.
        I change bedding of dried pee.
   This morning I cut hot dogs into penguins
        for a bento box.   Imagine.

    Who handles pecking order, ever?   Except
    the highest pecker?   Even as I think this
I'm sort of livened by   the destruction of her words.
Even as my mind darts away, finds shelter   outside the window
        in the pine grove—
    I love how, around my daughter's bedtime,
    the birds chirp into the innocuous twilight.
   At a certain point, some signal
   whisks them up en masse
        just above our treeline. I'm always listening for
        the sonic code so I'll know when to look, but it's unclear
        if it comes from beak or wingbeat.
            And now the live cloud: how do they
        keep from dispersing, how do they watch
        where they're flying, how do they not bump each other?

Sometimes they scatter.
         In fright?   Is there one dystopic bird
                              whose single feather-tremble
                              makes the cipher flip?
My beloved girl is tapping spoon against steel bowl.
    She wants more.
              She can't read it yet,
                   the silence and the window
                        into which my reflection pours.
                        My likeness offers more pudding,
                        heaves up a smile.
              Just watch for the cloud,
    the reorganising swarm,   and the pecking
        coming for the heart.

On the Resourcefulness of Others

I am not tending to my fire.
I am not tending to it, and in the absence
of my tending, the neighbour has taken
up the floorboards from my porch
and used them in her fire.
I love my neighbour.
I admire her resourcefulness.
But I regret my neglected porch, hanging
dumbly below the door jamb.

All Hands on Deck

We're driving to day camp across the river when she asks why
Eleanor Rigby keeps her face in a jar by the door.
Last week this sweet child folded and Japanese-stitched
a book for me. The ink smelled like apples,
the cover read: *POMES INSID!*
As if that makes it so, I thought.
Yesterday, she wrote on the kitchen chalkboard: *Weys*
to Hepl: cleen CAT liter!
Though her spelling is delinquent, I should explain to her
the face, the jar, the door. But how to answer when she sees poetry
as paper stitch and title page
or my silence behind a closed office door?
Synecdoche? No—image. Image is the place to start.
Indecision, my sister says, is my deficiency, and also maybe B12,
but meanwhile, from the car seat in perfect pitch
comes *Eleanor's jar by the door holds a face—*
Last night, this child sat at her tiny desk to write a comic book
entitled *The Feld and The Sond.*
The Sound and the Fury, I corrected, my patience
decayed after pyjamas and brushed teeth.
I can't always lock it down, my critical eye, my tone.
A month ago, my first mammogram was a pain.
Not a lot to grasp, hey? I joked.
The technician made a face. She'd heard that one before.
She looked at my chart and pinched my fullness flat
into fact. Did her face represent the whole
of her job? I felt weak in her hands, smelling so antiseptically
beyond reproach. When she looked away, I knew
I'd wanted too much for us to be on the same deck,
to be reassured that she too was scouting out the grey shadows
on the screen, making sure we were all harmless, all safe.

STILL FULL OF ARROWS

The Widening

In I suppose a pinprick of hope, I look out his windshield
wanting it to be true: northern lights or meteor showers
or something above the valley so his hand
on my thigh has a better explanation, anything but
the trope of furniture-maker/rig-driver driving his babysitter home
and stopping the car in the ditch. At two in the morning,
the black map of pinpoints above can be joined to form bears
and ladles of milk, archers with arrows pointing to North, to Hercules.
But his hand is on my thigh, same hand that leaves porn magazines
for me between the couch cushions, leaves cereal and sour milk, leaves
the nails of his children dirty and grasping for their one shared
toothbrush. I squint into the distance above the hills. If I want someone
to be grateful for me, I don't know it yet. If I want
a man's hand on my jeans, I don't know it yet. He decides
to point to a series of dots above us. And among the voices in my head
I hear him saying, *See? This is a kind of map.* And I don't hate him
for showing me that because yes, I see it too, it's a mess.

Albert County Breeder

It was years before I could walk back
to that doorway, figuratively hold

the post of your fallen porch
with its thousand green Mason jars

staring out towards the weathered barn.
On each window your dust

held the shapes of the cobwebs. Here
is your father coming out the kicked door.

Inside I've seen the hard-packed dirt
on your kitchen floor, ketchup caked

to the spoons, the bucket in the corner,
a.k.a. the winter toilet.

Outside we have more in common: bus shelter
for the wait at the end of the lane, broken-looking

crab apples, blue spruce, red pines,
tar shingles on the coop,

and the wild eyes in the animal
we brought to breed with your animal.

A White Tent Goes Up

What brings me to the empty pasture
across from the tomb they use
when the ground's too cold to dig?
It isn't the wooden poles' creak where joined at an apex
or the sun pushed into white canvas
or the women fanning their skirts
against their shame. I'm pushed by a crowd
of other children into an aisle, I feel too much skin
on the cold metal seat of a folding chair.
By the pulpit, Carter Bagley floats smugly
behind the drum kit. And in her slippery blouse,
training bra visible on shoulder bones,
Paula says, *I feel the Spirit.*
Someone shouts, *Amen.*

Which weighs more, dead body
frozen or unfrozen? It's the kind of question
I want answered. Yesterday, my father sent me to collect
docked lambs' tails in the clover. Five cents a tail.
The weight of them collected in my plastic bread bag.
What did you do for currency in your father's eyes?
Bread into fishes, bread into wine, what's revelation
is the first time I bear witness to the lamb
still inside its pink sac, swinging like wet grey rope
from the vulva of the ewe. Revelation is this lamb transforming
with apricots into stew on rice. Revelation is clotted
cream churning to butter, cheese hanging in its cloth
on the doorknob, the streams of yellow whey.
I haven't heard much from the preacher,
but the sweat on his cheeks

is pure biology.

I cannot lie: I'm scared I'll feel you, Spirit.
So show yourself to me.

Troy

I love Troy and I carve his name in the blond oak of the pew
and wait at the phone booth for his bus.

As it passes by, I find his window silhouette,
exquisite throat, delicate Adam's apple.

I give away so little of myself when I visit his house,
and as long as I wear T-shirt over swimsuit, place an ice pack

on the baby brother's swollen gums and wash the bacon pan,
I can even slide into Troy's pool and do laps.

I come up for air and every fibre of a curtain in the upstairs window
undulates with Troy. From the filter I remove leaves so wet

they disintegrate on touch. His mother strokes the lace on the velvet elbows
of her chair and says, *Bedroom Eyes here wants to sit with you in church.*

I come through the back gate in the morning, hoping.
On the long bench of atonement, she hands me the baby brother.

While Reverend Bagley peers through his bouquet of plastic tulips
on the pulpit, Troy looks straight ahead. But I know inside him

there's a horse. The horse will be unbridled if we speak.
I run across the backyard. I run past the church.

At the diamond, I run up the mountain of trembling bleachers to oversee
the red sand paths between first and second base.

Far off on the sidelines the parched observers see my wooden walls.
They don't see what's inside me, what it will do for Troy.

What Are You Waiting For?

When I lit the fire on its eastern edge
I didn't know how quickly the field would burn.
Without a ring of rocks to contain the sparks,
I cooked my foil envelope of potato and green beans.
From the brush I cut an aspen branch
to pierce and roast marshmallows.
I dowsed the flames and walked home,
leaving the field charred with new minerals.
The field had no comment.
After my strike it pushed seeds of bur oak,
knit wild doilies of carrot. In the wet slash
of the drain ditch, it interlaced clover and vetch
into a sort of covering and consented
to the spikes of irises rising sharp
through sludge. The morning sun wilted
buffalo grass, timothy, but it was not enough.
Today, wild peas and lupins, lupins, lupins—

But these are just another phase. Eventually
white cedar and fir will overtake them. Some would say
the field is disfigured. The field says it forgets
who struck what mineral against another mineral,
says it forgets all but that spark laid bare
on the flat palm of its clearing.
And it's hungry to be marked again
by that kind of danger. I see it starving
for an unexpected strike in the spot by the river
where the fireweed sprouts madly.

The Heart Speaks

I asked for the love that you wanted to ask for
I didn't know
but I knew I could get what I asked for

I had what you wanted
I had an ease with the asking   I'm sorry
I had it so easy
for me to ask for what you wanted so badly
what I hardly wanted at all

I asked

and you hated my ease

                    you are still full of arrows for me

how I went for
how I plucked him   because I could

it was nothing
                    as soon as I had him, I threw him away
like a wrapper he fell like a wrapper

and you hated my ease

you are not full of arrows for him though he took
what I threw out everywhere
with such ease

I am asking   it's been years since
what you wanted so badly
fell away but still   my tongue not his tongue is an arrow
inside your cheek

I Believe You Still Have My Key

You don't live inside me anymore, I think as I run past cigarette can,
deadwood bench, the man with his too-large tongue hanging out.

I am not proud of how I treat him, looking past his smoking shroud
of need, doing nothing with my thoughts but thinking:

Could be better, could be sweeter.
My excuse? Somewhere around fifteen, wit closed me

safely as a dress seam. Or fear. Same thing.
Inside were sealed all those reminders

not to live too much in my ideas, to slip inside your plans instead.
A halfway house should be called a waiting house, you once said.

I bit myself around the nails to let you out.
I was like those fields I've seen recuperating in clover

after years of potatoes. At the corner of my street,
the man with the tongue hangs out in his waiting house.

He's trying to live a little while he waits and he tells me to try it too:
Live a little—I run past his smoulder, run past your smoulder,

feeling it all, saying little. As for the other words, they sift
right through my pockets. They're only grit between my thighs.

Sonnet in Waiting Room

He's not allowed beyond the clinic's hall.
He turns and shrugs, what can he do? You spill
your purse, walk through metal detector, line
up at a glass screen to pay and sign to
enter this room. Bolted chairs and posters
are letters from a future to be planned
with someone less indifferent. Across the aisle
holding *Star* magazine, her flip-flops crossed like shields:

it's your younger self. And this room is a psalm
about erasing a mistake. From the purse
you take your paperback of shame.
You're thirty-five. Again you've fallen.
It pinches as it's taken out. But you love a good rebirth.

Against Confession

My daughter won't remember me asking the dog to sit, and how—
plunk, in the scratched bit of garden between barnyard
and doorway—she obeyed instead. Her memory winds in other ways,
magnificently obscuring facts. When my sister visits, she says I'm the same
because I don't remember what she swears she witnessed—
someone doing something to me in a bathroom long ago.
I go back, I inch along the tree bough, pick open the medicine bundle
of my mind: I see gold-leaf wallpaper, ceramic sink, teak shutters
with knobs I slid open and closed. I don't tell her that,
constructed well, forgetting slips things neatly where they're meant to go.

Forgetting slips neatly where it's meant to go. Constructed well, I slide
what I can't remember open then close it up. To my mind, there was
leaf wallpaper, sliding slats on shutters, holding knobs in a bathroom.
It's only gold and ceramic, for me. But my sister says my facts
are all magnificently obscured. My memory is my medicine, I bundle
around myself, inching backwards off the bough. In the garden between
barnyard and doorway, in the scratched bit of grass, I sit with my sister
as my child runs in her diapers. I want to change the subject. I tell the dog
to sit. My daughter won't remember what it was she was obeying.

How It Worked

On Avenue du Parc the editor presses me against the glass door
of a lobby. His golden drinks still glide liquid and careless in my belly.
I duck past his mouth. *Your apartment upstairs*, he whispers.
The delicate thing I thought we'd fashioned snaps in two.
I pull the door closed. Outside on the stoop, I see him draw open
his Italian coat. He removes the tool he knows well how to use.
We don't need to see more to know that he honed it. He honed it.
At his next poker game, my name's thrown down on the green field
of the table. It isn't a card or a chip that's worth much.
It's just under advisement: *She's not brave enough for my liking.*
Like that, I'm a payment reversed, I'm a fire in the groin going cold.

Falling in Love

A small brown vial from an Internet
company called Philosophy.
I shook it. I opened and tipped it
solidly against my pinkie. I placed my pinkie
into the divot under my nose.
Every morning, I dabbed on the potion
from that brown bottle. I believe my philosophy
was that I, like a midnight bus upstate,
could come through the dark forest of singleness
and wake up in Love. Then it actually worked—
Love walked up to my barstool, shook hands
with the locked gate of my unkempt apartment.
When it wined me and dined me, when
it crawled through my window at dawn
and broke the condom inside me—
it wasn't fireworks. More like
Love left me lying too long in the sun.
Now, the vial is gone. I take long baths
and drink too many glasses of wine
and pretend I've got no plans
once again.

Octopus Laser

At the time of my crime, I was a lover
who professed to love you even as I stole from you.
You were a lover who was often flexing in the mirror.
When you left for a lab where you studied the body,
I had all day to walk around the unpacked boxes
of your neighbourhood. I ate cans of your tuna-in-water
to keep my figure and rifled through your desk.
In one drawer, I found a laser pointer
with a button hidden in its sleek side. When I clicked,
a red octopus appeared on your bedroom wall.
I stole it.
          This is the easy part, to admit this
long after you've forgotten me. I slipped your laser
in my bra cup; without underwear, I pulled on my shorts.
I walked around the block thinking The Lover Who Leaves You
Too Long Alone. The Lover Who Buys Only Tuna.
And me, The Lover Who Loses Weight So Suddenly
She Doesn't Recognise Herself. Who is that philosopher
with the atoms, with the cheese? The one who cut squares
into tinier squares until he could no longer see
what he was cutting? Never mind. If I left in five minutes,
I could make the train: Manhattan, Poughkeepsie, Hudson, Montreal,
where people spoke a new language and didn't know
that I held in my pocket the piece of you that proved
I'd been to the big league once, leaned from those porch railings, waiting
for the Lover Who Never Came Home.
I wanted you to call. I wanted the packing boxes, tuna stink,
your sex on that dirty bed. Me and the thing you'd owned
spent months like this: wanting and pushing
the sleek button to bring the octopus swimming across
my bathroom wall, across the lip of the tub to my thighs.

Who is the philosopher who couldn't see the atom
and named the problem not him but the thing
he was cutting? I held the octopus in its secret place
until it went into a drawer. Even now, when I open the drawer,
I see you. Useless with your old batteries,
still mine. It's pristine, this thought,
even as my skin sheds, the past rewords itself,
my atoms double and double.

Stun Guns

I don't know if the pigeon was stunned
from hitting the patio door or from her torn-open
breast, but while my husband held her wings,
I saved her by crossing twine around her throat
and tightening until her lavender lids met,
her black keratin beak parting.

Sometimes I am hungry suddenly
and I don't know how you stop yourself, but I can't
and I eat the butter and the bread, I eat the olives
like popcorn and my body won't keep much of it,
but it keeps enough so that I'm not the one
you look at anymore. But who thinks
their body is the one you look at
until it is the one, or who thinks their body is the one
to be used until it is. You placed my hand
under your bed covers and told me I made you like this,
I did this to you
when I only walked into your room
looking for my beer.

I think of my own daughter
picking up our cat after it died,
carrying its tortoise-fur body into the kitchen
to ask what was wrong.
I told her the cat was gone.
She'll never stop crying in my head—

the cat is gone, the pigeon gone, but that girl who opened her throat
to your beer funnel at your so-called monastery?
She's here with all your butter.

FLOWERS FOR ALL OCCASIONS

Then

found poem, Mommy's journal

the ducks would rise from the river
the sky would darken
the birds would stop singing
the smoke would come in at the windows
the cake would fall in the middle
the dog would be lost
the dishes would never get done
the grass would turn into wildflowers
the rocks would pile at the edge of the water
the crows would find him

The Rising Action

My mother's brazen germination: the doctor's son
flirting with the kitchen help. He pocketed her hand, jimmied the girl

through the back door, walked her backward
to the barn. In the breezeway, the playfulness

went south. It took her breath away, his shameless lifting
of the apron, the skirt.

My mother was the rough idea that insisted on thriving
up the backstairs, over a kitchen: a dark-loving plant in a basket.

My mother was coal smoke, rickets,
dirty bibs, a stroller missing a wheel and sinking

as the tide came in. I know her name
changed three times. I know the date and place of birth,

not much more. But in the black dust of her moods,
she took me back to that foundling house.

I saw why the breadknife was sometimes
at the ready. I know enough:

you leave a room, you look over your shoulder.
You find a white stone in the sand, you ask for what you need.

Then throw it in the air.

Wild Exile

She stops the car in the red dirt
in front of a house that could be the house,
could be doorknob, clothesline, craggy grey shingles
where she spent her third year.

Nothing is different from her memory, but nothing
is the same either. A picture of a house
is not a real house.

She walks down to the brook,
which is where she left it. When she slides her feet
into the cool tawny water, she tries to put things
back into place, but a mink darts
under a tree root, catfish wind themselves
darkly upstream, and all the birds go silent,
pretending to be leaves. Nothing here for her.

Now the house, its hill, even her car
huddle suddenly into shadow,
a great cloud folding over a valley.
But under her feet the water has cleared,
the stones bare as a winter floor—
What's there to cry about? *House,*
your floors were so cold.

At the Foundling Home

found poem, Mommy's journal

there were always little children you could hug
and older children who'd touch you.

Back to the Land

I asked what happened to her.
She answered obscurely: board to nail,
nail to board. She knew what she knew and she bound it
in thread. Around that she bound twine. She crumpled it
like paper and with a match made her tinder.
She added bark, snapped kindling, then softwood,
and one chunk of hardwood with a burl.
In the kitchen, she cut what she knew
from an animal belly, leaving a firm strip of fat.
When she roasted it, blisters formed
and dripped in the ash. In the flames on its skin
she saw leaps and retractions. She ate her fill
and there wasn't a word about love.
When she couldn't sleep, she sat in the basement
tending furnace and fire. She coiled wool round
her palms. She took tacks from the box in the drawer
and punched better stories into the frame on quilt blocks.
She matched calico to chintz: hearts for dots,
cubes for tulips. With a needle, she took to the cloth,
edging diamonds and pinwheels.

Sometimes she looked through me
and said words no one could love.
Afterwards, she climbed under her quilt
and slept back to back with what happened.
In the morning, she cut oatcakes
into squares. She fed what she knew, forked timothy
into its trough. She pulled the teats for the milk,
lay her cheek against the flank of the beast
and closed her eyes. She felt something
like love. It felt stiff as horsehair.
She pulled it across her barn doors

and she plucked it. The sound was far-fetched.
I believed it.

Lambing Season

She slept against hay bales the nights
when a ewe was in labour. Sometimes she slept
in the feeders, in the chaff,
surrounded by bodies of sheep, breathing and bleating.

I want you to know that her farm is still
in that valley, along roads barbed with dried mud.
I want you to know I did not want
a mother who wore barn boots. I spread out

so gamely my wishes; I had all the chances.
And here comes regret: it's me in the feeder tonight.
I wait and I watch the ewe and her heaving. I clear
the breach, I pull out the lamb. By the back hooves

I swing her through the air and she breathes.

Wedding in Rimouski

The tent fly whipped
in the wind. A slap to the face.
My mother was just there at the campfire
handing us yogurt cups, peeling back foil
to show us the daisy cake she called lazy.
Her whipped cream came from no can.
She milked it herself. She milked and she milked
and now I see how we all milked the moment
that weekend, skimming the cream, pretending
that the throbbing at the base of her skull was just
a hair, ingrown on the back of her head.
On her way to the dance floor she lost her balance,
but we were cutting her cake and her cream,
someone struck their spoon to a glass,
the groom played ukulele and sang with the bride.
At some point there was swimming.
In the rowboat, my mother wobbled, applying lotion
to my father's cheeks. Under her kerchief,
one hair grew inward. A single hair
growing unstoppably fast.

Juice

Juice pressed from the beet, cabbage we've heard makes a dent
in the cells, multitudes tripling, humming through lymph,

through her mutinied spleen, her liver's dark shelf.
All six of us at a loss. It's true what I've known

all along: we're not safe in numbers. On the back porch
we murmur to neighbours, *If this doesn't work, we'll sell, maybe*

fly her to the panhandle, someone says there are tonics or injections,
turmeric—*stop talking, she's here,* stomping in

from the rhubarb-scented
garden where she gets away from our fretting

to do what? We don't know. We have this juice,
will she drink? Her jagged shoulder blades drop.

She takes one sip to please us.
We step back in unison and imagine this liquid

transformed as a swarm on the map of her lymph
to her spine, a staircase of ivory and blood work,

where the numbers are not good. No safety in numbers.

The Dress
found poem, Mommy's journal

I am like a dress—
a clean dress
over a terrible wound.

The dragging of a belly
across gravel
is under my dress.

It Comes Back

Pain has its value. It wakes her up,
twists its pink yoke at her neck,

reminds her to be fearful when necessary.
It vies with the grey sinew

of her calf muscle, pinches the blood.
She limps around it, holds tight

to what she made of herself, parses it
like rules, like squares of toilet paper

allotted to each of her children.
She climbs the hill from the garden.

What advice is handed from mother
to mother? When blending pastry,

use ice. Prick names into pies with a fork.
As for pain, you bear it

as it courses through your neck.
As it clinches your liver as hardy

as parsley, built like the cabbages
squatting in the chill.

Dénouement

When she loved me, she got on with it
in silence: she punched down the bread and salvaged
the cold oatmeal on the stove.

It wasn't what I asked for.

Near the end, I help her off the toilet—
so light and mean.
She grazes a fist against my leg.
Leave me, she says.

There, there—
I'm speaking to a meadow about its chaff.
Why bring up the clover.

Flowers for All Occasions

On the Prime Care bed in the living room
it's time to say goodbye. *Too soon to say for sure,*

I tell the limboing silence and the shroud
who is still my mother.

I am also a kind of chrysalis. I tuck the word
pregnant behind her ear.

I'm guilty of something
even as I run the pink sponge-pop of moisture

around her lips, even though I've changed
her pyjamas and her diaper, administered to her chest port

the drug that supports the freezing illusion
that we are both sitting outside of time: she's not leaving,

I'm not leaving. It's still good
to hold her hand on this bedsheet.

I pretend I am a membrane
through which she could pass

to forgive me for wanting also to be recognized
as someone changed by life.

The Falling Action

She was sixty-nine or was it seventy? Some people said a ripe old age.
It's said that if the young learn that they are dying, they become holy.
I suppose it's their face. It is said, anyway. Above the barn sink,
the glass held the reflection of a barn cat leaping for a barn swallow.
I saw it go down, slapped my wet hands
and seethed: *Shit! Well, that's over.*

I looked everywhere for meaning: in her pyjamas,
in her somewhat-holy face. I read poems to her that were little stories:
man walks into autumn beach town, is a skunk, finds a skunk, the end.

I made lemon custard. I set spoons on the two-by-four table.

I pushed in her Puritan bench. The other side of the window
bloomed lilac—I can't say what I want that to mean—
still I brought a bowl to her table. She spat spoonfuls into the napkin,
her face lit with adoration for that later-place. She made a device
of folding her napkin into smaller squares, hiding my love without looking.
But who can talk about what you will miss
every minute? *We turned toward signs painted Peaches,* I recited.

Once she looked up and said, *I'll miss that face*—I
keep combing the moment. It was said.
I return to it—anything could happen.

The News

I placed the telephone in the cradle
and did not stop walking

until I was lying
under a cave of trees in a stranger's yard.

I lay there like a wide lake.
I didn't have the deep thoughts

of a lake. Instead, I had the modest thoughts
of a mother:

> *I am the lake if you want me to be the lake.*
> *I can also be the kept lawn or this cedar shrub.*
> *Even the roses, which I dislike. Or disliked*
> *before I became them.*

Mink Attack

We left as soon as we heard. Pre-dawn we crossed the border, almost all
still unbelievably alive and highway aiming, gritty tires churning us on.
Mid-morning, we arrived. At her back-door post, my sister greeted us.
Days and days and days, we tended what absence could look like so long
we thought we knew. But it wasn't like that. The back door, kicked tough
and often, gone soft in its wooden panel. The living room swept, crank bed
undone, packed in the quiet ambulance. We'd let go of the pyjamas and
the body. We'd kept gold rings, her incongruous assembly of pink teacups,
casual toss of wood to woodpile, sensual hip-thrusting walk in rubber boots.
Now our gaze falls on the path, past rosebush, onwards
to dwarf cherry—not looking so good, bark stripped with heart rot—
and the henhouse beyond it. My sister is out there
on the flagstones in socks. She clutches her own elbows. Her face less cool
than on our last visit. New sister, remember that time the pullet got pulled
from the lay box. We watched her go limp in that animal's pink mouth.
Those left in the house were no longer pullets.

You Can't Take It with You

I don't like the velvety drapes,
the posters of waterfalls, lone paths in forests,

single footsteps in sand. In the dim room, you're wearing
my old pyjamas.

When they leave me with your body, I put my head
on the dark room of your chest.

I hear old words fighting in my head. I've made these mistakes—
Leave them with me, you say. *I'll use them as rags.*

As a Pigeon in Its Dovecote

I walk through the house,
closing the doors to the rooms

that are clean. The blender and glass,
the teacup and saucer washed.

The jagged vase is out of place,
so I push it right.

The rooms I can't close up
I turn my back on.

I sweep the front walk, pull weeds
from the dust and throw them

without a thought
off the edge of the earth.

The neighbour's dog is large
and often its poop bags

are left on my stoop.
One problem is I say nothing.

When she was alive, I called my mother
to complain about things like this.

I'd tease her about her poetry too,
Is your house tidy enough

to write in? Now our conversation
is this strange appliance

I still try to speak through.
Don't think it brings her closer.

It just fills the space
where the unhaunted waste time.

The Art of Waiting

It's the same everywhere, but here we wait outside the bodega
for our mothers to return. We sip our coffee in paper cups,
balance our toes on the edge of the first step littered
with newspapers we pretend to read
until they come for us. The first through the door
isn't mine, she's dressed wrong, firewoman-like,
red straps across her chest. One is in her housecoat
carrying her dew-covered mail.
One is all business, in uniform, hairnet to keep stray hairs in place.
Sometimes they change it up, the mothers
delayed for days or hours, or they end up coming
from another direction entirely, or only one appears,
looking like a nun, grey-habited, rumpled, the headpiece askew.
Sometimes they're more selfish than we remember.
They've forgotten nickels or peanut-butter cup totems
to show they thought of us while they were gone.
Instead they flash girlhood wishes: an armful of dolls
in pillbox hats, a tan pony with a bridle.
My mother will be easy to spot: matchbox of seashells
tucked beneath her white wing, her laugh inked
pinpoint by pinpoint into the drums of my ears.
The wait becomes endless. Each time more mothers come
swiftly through the tinkling door, our throats leap.
See our grim foundling smiles, see the flowers we picked
from the cracks in the sidewalk? We're so ready to hand over
these bright bits of gratitude for our mothers in return.
But now the sidewalk darkens. Mine won't laugh
to find me out so late. Sure enough, her silhouette's approaching,
marching grimly, a little unfamiliar in slippers and kimono.
But that's her smell: woodsmoke, hay mow.
And without delay she corrects my sweater buttons.
Takes my shoulders and fixes my eyes to hers.

Oh, how I sift myself joyfully back into her grasp
and her shushing, *Didn't I tell you?*
Be still, don't move, stay in one place!—
and I'm trying to get words out,
trying to tell her, *I did it, I do it, I'm doing just that.*

The End

I've been saying it for years now on the last page of every story—
The end, The end, they sing as they toddle to bed.

When she could no longer leave her bed
I gave my mother a gingko in a plastic bucket. I was thinking

she might plant it. I wasn't thinking. The papered leaves
turned yellow and fell off suddenly one night.

A Pollyanna principle is love with all you have
and the love will return. But my mother's face

was silent and stainless as a sink. The glass of water
at the bedside was full because she didn't drink.

I close the book. My second-born is asking if it's the end.
It hardly bothers me to look into eyes so like my mother's and lie.

The Saving of Things

found poem, Mommy's journal

The flowers are not real
but when I thought they were,
and that a hand had put them there
for my pleasure, I felt happy.

THE HEIRESS

On Being a Sculptor

On his last visit, my father uses the good knife to cut oranges for breakfast.
We go see Henry Moore at the museum, recline on the upholstered bench.
The guard turns. My father runs his hand over marble buttocks
and why not. We have beer and a dessert.
He signs the guestbook *Kilroy was HERE*
and gently nudges my daughter's face into the drinking fountain.
I'll go get ice cream, he says. Meaning he wants me to go.
He peels a twenty, then farts and leaves the room
to be with my mother in a gallery only the dead can visit.
A large man, he swallowed bread and cream when everyone
and no one looked. I miss the wooden steeples
of his knuckles folded on my table. Sometimes he returns
to check that my patio is made of cedar,
which smells lovely as it greys and will never rot.

Room 317, Chateau de Champlain

At the end of the day, to walk
whatever dog out into the field.

Even when he didn't have a dog,
even when there was no field to think in

because when the farm sold,
he lost his field, his dog.

He lost rye grass, the base of each stem
he used to bite flat for its sweet centre.

Even the spittle foam. Even shredded chaff—
how could we have given up

his Rhodes grass
and let him end like that,

toppled, heart stopped, in that bed.

A Visitation

I stepped into Dorval Airport,
one middle daughter bringing death certificate

to cheery ticket counter attendant,
through security line to jump seat.

Transported over the white lions of clouds,
I think I prayed, *Show yourself to me.*

And expected you to do it.
Below me, my old brown-mouthed bay,

the power plant still the same white disk.
I love you, I said. *Please blind me*

in your deflected light. Around it the spruce as dark
as your younger beard. All that time

you'd watched me wasting the peach of my youth,
you'd said nothing. In those black trees,

I needed the surprise of an enflamed object
to be a barn and nothing else.

I concentrated everything into a neat
square around its brightness and it became a barn.

Tell Me What to Do

The pebbles hurt our feet. We popped seaweed pods
with our thumbs. We waded in the icy bay, dove into the next wave
and came up with more seaweed on our arms.
It rained. We were drunk on scotch

                        when one sister, certain
the lone sea duck on the waves was you, began to cry.
Our teeth clenched when we shouted goodbye to it
so she'd feel less alone.

Sometimes you'd call down through the vent from the upstairs toilet
to bring you more paper. From there, your view
                        across the jerseys' upper field
was obstructed a little by the nest under the eave
filled to brooding with swallows.

It meant something
            that you let me drive you home that last time.
At the mailbox, your finger jabbing left
against the windshield   until I turned the wheel.

The Heiress

He had the acuity to slide his smoothest pen
into his breast pocket so I couldn't steal it.

Nine days later, his heart gave out. At the funeral,
I could not stop crying, could not

be trusted. I slipped out to use the toilet.
No, I told my thieving fingers: I slipped out

to raid his bureau, to slip into my wallet
his ripped boarding pass, folded

into a plane. His miniature bronze pitcher
pushed its sharp spout in my palm but

it didn't stop me. I deserved
his noise-cancelling headphones

and my story of his story of rickshawing
past the Taj Mahal. It was my baby sister

who found his body fallen
half out of bed. I've been told the coroner

pronounced the time. Everyone got something.
So I'm heavy with my objects, smug

with my pen, already framed
in glass and hung.

Fox's Sleep Revisited

She wants my hens.
Hunger makes her small-waisted
as a wasp. Mid-afternoon, voracious,
she slips by the verandah to attack the cat
and the grosbeaks in the feeder.
But really she wants the hens,
so silent in the shed they must smell her.
In the morning, four feathers on a fence post,
Swiss dots of blood and musk.

Woolf Digression

Each time Woolf turned a page, the words bored her.
She thought, there's a chance here

                     for surprise
and then no surprise.

She could not take another last page,
not another syllable, she could not stop

the wishful voice of the scissor, the penknife,
its gleaming eye tooth.

Me, I see the corner of a page like a mouth
asking for its bed covers to be turned down, a voice

under the pillow: *You are what loves you
not what you love.*

I still have eyes, Woolf said. She could not stop the new
keen love for the speckled pinks, greys, the liver red

of stones. It didn't seem unreal, this river
and love.   It looked real.

When I tell this story to an intern in a lab coat,
I can see I scare her.

You are what you love, she corrects me.
She thinks she corrects me.

She writes on her pad, hands me the page.
There's no surprise: swallow with water until

it looks real, until it gets real,   what you love.

Chance Harbour

Some things cannot be faced head-on. Inside
the tide mark, men in boots come with clam shovels.
They scrape the ocean floor. The thoughts I can't lose

or use spout from the sanded throats of clams beneath
what the tide exposes. Two years after your death, you're back—
visiting my sister's yard, admiring the lilacs. Some things cannot

be faced head-on. When the men climb into a dinghy, they each accept
a black mask and plunge for prickled urchins to be eaten, peeled,
by wealthy Asian men. What if I lose these thoughts

beneath the bay's smooth skin, where low tide holds its copper strength
for only sixty seconds? I have no time to fix you in place before
you're gone. Some things cannot be faced head-on.

This visit, you stand by those lilac flutes, unruffled
bay behind you. All pettiness aside, I can't be the daughter
pulling something hopeful from my thoughts. I must never lose

you, but are we allowed a break? Now on the peeling rust stones,
the tide stops—nothing to heed. Farther out, the black suits dive
for gold. Some things cannot be faced head-on.
What I can't lose, I've used.

Nor Do I Want To

Don't you know
grass blades don't
hold hands. They slide
past each other like
breezes do. Without
even the whisper
of recognition.

Valentine

I know what it means to farm honey—the work
of building the frame, the stapling of combs.
I know the waiting. It's the pencil I place by my bed.
It's the cat waking me with his kneading for milk
where there's no milk. When there's a swarm, I'll find
courtiers in the apple blossoms. With the glove, I sweep away
the scout bees. And when I see my broody queen,
I place her in the cell cup and wait.

I think of my father, how he slid each scraped frame
into the extractor. He spun the wooden handle until his arms ached.
Why in the basement? Why the dank mire by the furnace?
I didn't ask. Maybe effort is blind—just muscles at work in the dark.
No, no, something answers, its voice sweet to remind me
of amber flying from the paddle to stick on the walls of plastic.

JOY IN THE CLOISTERS

Overheard at the Sports Centre

Stop your hip from poking my hip. I can feel you doing it. I haven't eaten
since last night. It's the soap thing in the women's washroom again.
I'm afraid he's not back from lunch yet. I might end up a record holder
for most time on this bench. Don't look so sad. We have a system.
I go like this with my hand to my daughter and it means okay.
She goes like that and means five minutes. You have to be invited.
Hair like that, thick as horsetail, takes forever with the dryer.
That was quick. I like her but not for two hours straight. If you can stand it,
you're laughing. Can you move your bag? I think the dryer is a silver nose
in a white old-lady bonnet. Why did the woman say, *Excuse me?*
Excuse me? at her baby's face? Is Keto a dog's name? Never actually gone in
and looked. She's a real person when she smiles. How do you do it?
I'm living on croissants at the moment. Almost took my fingers off.
I'm still nuts about him. You'll need a key to access a locker. It's garbage,
the difference between peewee and novice. I know more about this than
I'm prepared to say. Going for groceries is code for disappearing.
Whoever is on the ice sounds angry. I feel like doing it myself.
Don't watch my phone over my shoulder. Go play. Go play, please. Look,
ma'am—it is ma'am isn't it? What you thought was a dead bird
is actually a trash bag.

The Residency

I'll be waiting for a train, or floating along a moving sidewalk
between flight and baggage claim, offspring from a newer love firmly
in my thoughts. You'll touch my elbow in the coffee line: *Remember me?*

There'll magically be time to talk—new world dictator,
same old regime, dipping interest at the bank, and roof repair—
before I tell you my cat from the Chinese grocery

died ten years ago. Before she withdrew all sweetness,
her eyes said how much it hurt to leave. I felt this too keenly,
I've been told. Remember the bedsheets we didn't have to wash.

My wariness about wine at lunch. Dinner waiting on us at the table.
I hid what I wanted most for fear you'd feel it. I still have your gift,
driftwood that looked like a stone.

It isn't stone. It doesn't recognize itself in this new home.

Blanche

You flirt, of course, with the husband.
Eyes fluttering, an old game.

Before you know it, the valise is wide open,
spread on the taut, gaunt frame of a story

where there's no real story.
It's all rah-rah. It's pumped blood.

The heart being a thing that can mean everything
and nothing, a figurative opening

emboldened when you mix it
in a glass with rum. Mid-January

no longer stern. Not much later, you wake up.
In the mirror is the squirrel's nest

dangling in the Y of a tree.

You Bring It Home with You

At dawn, the cat makes his break,
returns triumphant with the first nestling

held in his teeth like an empty change purse.
Barely grey, just fuzzy skin

around a pulse. I thrust the garden hoe
into its neck. Spank the cat. He runs inside

to kick more of his wilderness
into the sofa cushion.

Later, having bruised himself
into something more social,

he comes to chatter at my door
to see if I will bite. *I hear you*, I say.

But don't think I'm not buying
a new collar with a bell from the Dollarama.

On the way home, maybe I'll stop
at the CN rail yards to tear out some lilies

by their roots. An offering I'll place
beside his water bowl.

Supper Hour

It's a lit storm, a slick highway for stride bikes:
our daughters race around the kitchen island
where I laugh a little too hard, wield the knife
we bought together, slice the head off
broccoli for the thousandth time. I like to think
I have it down pat: metal handle, grim chop
through the rough stalks, my real self obscured
by this mother self, lip lines, hips pressed
firmly forward into the task. I've gotten used to
nuisance and delay, feel less abandoned
by the lights, the concrete and the jungle of my city
in which our house is archipelago, some new pact
with rigour. Yet I'm always longing for
what I remember as Café Open da Night,
my black book like a promise. I move persistently
through other vegetables—turnip, beet—
on into purple evening, the heft of knife, smack of steel.
This is a one-person job. I brush the husks and stems
below the counter, dimness broadening the kitchen.
The children forget I'm here. My corner of the room
is a shadow the hour creeps towards while outside
sparrows hang in undergrowth, the racoon picks along the fence
to watch me through the plate glass, and rush hour
beyond our street thickens with idling. I could cut it.
A knife chop is a sound to which everything surrenders.

The Standstill

We fought after the children
were in bed. We fought while scraping plates,

gathering glasses after the guests had gone. Sometimes
the fight was vapour, vanishing from the living room

when we came down for breakfast. Like you,
I believed there were words, maybe even a single

word, that would solve things. We searched for it.
I walked the football field, the dog straining against

its lead. You walked the dog where you walked it.
Before bedtime we cleaned our children's bodies.

We brushed their teeth quickly, leaving the rest
up to fate. I wanted to find that word, but

sometimes I came into the kitchen
as you left it and silence filled

every jar in the fridge. On these nights I waited in bed.
I breathed in the dark. I thought, maybe tonight

a child will crawl into our sheets, murmur our word
in her oblivious spread-eagle sleep.

Killing the Dream

Eggs pray for lightness as they slip out of their
shells into the whisk and business of my bowl.
Beer wants its sugar. Oatmeal wants its butter,
its moat of milk. Oh, the aloe prays
for some suffering, just a dab of it
to soothe and smooth, not smother.
I, this new mother, want nothingness—
and sugar, and silence, as did the mother before me
and before her, that mother wanted a visitor,
an engine grinding up her lane.
My sister pays me in bread to tell her
she's young and not bitter.
My other sister asks me to ignore her unhappiness,
which bubbles like a yeast, creeps toward me
as if I am warmth and air—
and my fending it off is a kind of prayer,
and it's starving.
The table prays to its cloth and congress of chairs.
My queen bed prays for emptiness
until that's all it is. Meanwhile,
my husband wishes to place his head
between my breasts.
Only bigger. But my whipped eggs
seek an empty heat behind the oven door.
This dishwasher melts the heart
of my plastic spoons. The dryer takes hair elastics,
and buttons and pins into shadowy heavens
I don't know but want to understand.
I also want to dog-paddle in a circle,
wanting for nothing. To climb out of water
the colour of labradorite and not even lean
forward to cover my waist.

I'm grimly praying the zucchini
will stop rotting. But the dog needs walking
and I'm her only leash. Someone has to be the brace
on my husband's knee, sit as the watch cap
on my girls. I carry the aloe to a more southern exposure
where it waits liquidly inside its green spikes.
Calamity keeps brewing on the basements steps.
It gurgles. But I'm so far from any lake.

In the Figurative Barn

It hurts to lose an eye to the jab of any horn.
When I come back home, my sister tells me
I am the horn.

To pay attention to what we can't see
is a waste, she says. Let's talk instead
of hens and shovels, let's talk the thorn bush

overgrowing in the pasture and what needs mucking
in the barn. I haven't lost my other eye, I see the pain
in her neck is me—

while she thinks I've wasted everything
on the figurative, I think she's lost her eyes
to many horns.

I dislike her chickens and the barn, its rakes
and stanchions in their row. I dislike the goats
with all their bleating and my sister

who doesn't pick off thorns so much now
as wire shut hen cages and milk goats. And make soap.
Making soap, my sister's hands are virtuous.

I wish I was so clean. I've lost my sister to a horn.
I miss her. I don't blame her for the wiring
of the cage.

From here, my view is of the pasture.
I sit in my bed of thorns, I toss my horns.
Against my neck, the stanchion clanks.

When in Pompeii

Not even daylight yet, just its intention.
Hesitation everywhere.
Moths cluster on the grey ocean
of a pothole.

Scientists call it selfish herding,
how the moths hover
before deciding where to hide
amongst each other.

There's this particular way I've found to feel
almost better. It isn't giving up.
I can't save all of myself. But perhaps

what is most precious might be
perhaps, perhaps preserved.

The Row House

When the dog comes home from her alley frontier
and you come pushing the gate, locking bike
to house or vice versa.

When our daughter plucks
the devil's paintbrush and sings, *Mommy loves,
Mommy doesn't love—*

I know it's time to hunker down and climb
the animal's back. It's grim.
I cannot speak of but do it.

Meanwhile, the cat collapses into herself,
curls her cloven hooks and grins.
What an empty promise

not to play with prey. When I stop wanting to be yours
will you still be mine? Please

bow like the reed when wet. And bend.
What time is there to dry.

Domestic Scene

The children call to us
Goodnight, Goodnight.

He doesn't ask for anything
from his side of the yoke.

A slap on his broad back,
he walks heavily into the door frame.

Within the bind, you could turn
and look him in the heart—

You could cup his beard
in your hand:

Let me lead you
to the field.

Darling Citizen

My feet suspend above the feathered milfoil of scum.
In the fingers of the willow a crane pauses.
Steady as the sweetflag, but with a better view, the crane doesn't ask
why I jump from simile to memory, recalling here on this black pond
my oldest sister's boyfriend, a fencer, who practiced his indifference
while I loitered on the lawn, combing his grass with my palms.
I'd say my memory of first love works okay here.
The heart knows what to do, what not to do again.
In earth years, my heart is ridiculously young.
It blinks closed, it glistens open to herd the blood.
It's the red eye waiting for the lunge.
It parts my reeds and silt and lifts me out.

Joy in the Cloisters

We are saved not because we are worthy.
We are saved because we are loved.

— Joy Williams

More than anything I want to take the anonymous subway
anonymously. But when the uniforms approach, I know
they're looking for me. If they're looking for my fraud
they'll find it. Everyone has something. But all I ever wanted
was to travel up to Inwood and touch the Unicorn Tapestry
and see the tapestry's hero running where she wants,
dipping her wild love into any old stream, her eager hooves splashing
before being stabbed in her pure heart and penned like a beast.
Lesson learned? The more we give, the more likely
we'll get nothing back. I was once like that—a taker, an owner
of fuck all cares. I refused interviews. No, I refused coffee dates
and interviews. Now it's the end, I'm past the turn.
In the gift shop and bookstore, I can tell you I stayed a long time,
turning over one book then another. Who wants to leave such a place?
I saw Joy Williams in dark glasses in her author photo.
Who wears dark glasses in an author photo. Who knows they're that pure.

NOTES

The epigraph is from Denise Riley's "A Shortened Set."

"Fox's Sleep" takes its title from the name for a state of apparent sleep (or feigned indifference).

In "A White Tent Goes Up" the term "docked" refers to the practice of removing part of a lamb's tail soon after birth to prevent disease or infection.

"What Are You Waiting For?" is for Sarah D.L.

"Octopus Laser" references Democritus, a pre-Socratic philosopher known for his formulation of an atomic theory.

"The Falling Action" references Li-Young Lee's "From Blossoms" and Robert Lowell's "Skunk Hour."

"Room 317, Chateau de Champlain" borrows from a letter Daphne Boxill shared with me.

"Valentine" is after Jean Valentine's "Bees."

"The Residency" is after Hendrik Rost's "You Here"—it is also for him.

"Darling Citizen" lifts its title from Mary Oliver. It is for Kellyanne and Mary.

ACKNOWLEDGEMENTS

Grateful acknowledgement is made to my mother, Elizabeth Venart, for "Then," "At the Foundling Home," "Wild Exile," and "The Saving of Things," which borrow directly or fold phrases from her journals.

I am also so grateful to the editors of *Concrete and River, The Malahat Review, The Moth,* and *Numéro Cinq,* in which some of these poems appeared in earlier drafts.

I couldn't have taken the time necessary to revise this collection without the support of the Canada Council for the Arts. Thank you.

Without prodding and encouragement from Cristina Lugo, Susan Gillis, Sue Elmslie, Kellyanne Conway, Mary Panke, Emily Venart, and Marge Piercy, I wouldn't have done anything but write these poems in my head. Thank you.

Thank you to Brick. Barry Dempster and the acquisitions team for seeing the poems in their roughness and saying yes. Kitty Lewis for sending me, all through my silent years, books and love and encouragement. Alayna Munce, I thank you and my poems thank you for your ear and eye (and your patience and grace when I could not make those impossible decisions). To Sue Sinclair, I loved every minute of working with you. You are such a tender and thoughtful poet and person and, I highly suspect, an incredible mother. Thank you for sandwiches, coffee, and explaining the sublime.

I wish to also thank everyone at U.N.I. for their understanding, when, mid lift, sprint, or plank, I was checked out, thinking of poems.

Laurie, Moley, Paul, Catherine, Yves, Umaia, Dottie, my sisters, my brother, and especially the loves of my life Mathieu, Olive, Alice, thank you for understanding me and loving me despite my thorns and horns.

SARAH VENART's poetry has been published in *The Moth Magazine, Numéro Cinq, Concrete and River, The New Quarterly, The Malahat Review, The Fiddle-head, This Magazine, Prism International*, and on CBC Radio. She is the author of *Woodshedding* (Brick Books, 2007) and a chapbook, *Neither Apple Nor Pear*. Sarah lives in Montreal.